WILLIAM K. DURR • JEAN M. LE PERE • MARY LOU A

CONSULTANT • **PAUL McKEE**

LINGUISTIC ADVISOR • **JACK E. KITTELL**

RAINBOWS

HOUGHTON MIFFLIN COMPANY • BOSTON

NEW YORK • ATLANTA • GENEVA, ILLINOIS • DALLAS • PALO ALTO

Acknowledgments

For each of the selections listed below, grateful acknowledgment is made for permission to adapt and/or reprint copyrighted material, as follows:

"Ants Live Here." Text copyright © 1967 by Lilian Moore. From *I Feel the Same Way*. Used by permission of Atheneum Publishers.

"Buzzy Bear and the Rainbow." From *Buzzy Bear and the Rainbow* by Dorothy Marino, copyright © 1962 by Franklin Watts, Inc.

"Cooking." From *Whispers and Other Poems*, copyright © 1958 by Myra Cohn Livingston. Reprinted by permission of Harcourt, Brace & World, Inc.

"I Wouldn't" from *You Read to Me, I'll Read to You* by John Ciardi. Copyright © 1962 by John Ciardi. Published by J. B. Lippincott Company.

"Little Raccoon and the Thing in the Pool." Adapted from *Little Raccoon and the Thing in the Pool* by Lilian Moore. Pictures by Gioia Fiammenghi. Copyright © 1963 by Lilian Moore and Gioia Fiammenghi. Used with permission of McGraw-Hill Book Company.

"Saturday Night" by Lois R. Pasley from *New Poems for Children*, reprinted by permission of Hart Publishing Company, Inc.

"Too Many Bozos" reprinted by permission from *Too Many Bozos* by Lilian Moore. © Copyright 1960 by Golden Press, Inc.

"Wait for a Windy Day" by Lilian Moore, adapted with the permission of the author.

Book cover, title page, and magazine covers by JOHN KUZICH.

Illustrators: WILLI BAUM (PP. 119–137), TOM COOKE (PP. 98–115), BARBARA DAVISON (PP. 22–40), ED EMBERLEY (PP. 43–56, 76–77), LOIS ELHERT (P. 142), BOB FRANK (P. 116), JOHN FREAS (PP. 41–42, 78, 117–118, 140–141, 162–165), TRINA SCHART HYMAN (PP. 7–21), ELAINE LIVERMORE (P. 192), DAVID MCPHAIL (PP. 81–96), SUSAN PERL (PP. 57–75), JOE VENO (PP. 138–139, 166–191), ERIC VON SCHMIDT (PP. 145–161).

Photographer: ERIK ANDERSON (P. 97).

Contents

GREEN RAIN

RED GOLD

BLUE GRASS

GREEN RAIN

GREEN RAIN

One Frog, Two Frogs

JOE: Do you know what I have in this box?

STEVE: Is it a toy?

Is it something funny?

JOE: It's not really funny.

But I have a lot of fun with it.

Take a look!

STEVE: I thought you had a toy in there.

But it's a real frog.

Where did you get it?

JOE: It's not a real frog.

It's a little toy!

I got it at the toy store.

9

STEVE: Your toy frog will be a lot of fun.

It looks just like a real one.

JOE: I just thought of something, Steve.

We can go find Betty and Sue.

And we can scare them with this frog!

Come on!

The Boys Find Betty

JOE: Hi, Betty.

I have a surprise in here.

I got it at the toy store.

BETTY: I like toys!

Will you let me see it?

JOE: That really scared her a lot.

She thought it was a real frog.

STEVE: That was fun!

She's going to Sue's house now.

She will tell Sue it's a real frog.

JOE: Let's put the frog back into the box.

We can really have some fun now.

JOE: Hi, girls.

What are you doing?

Can we come in?

BETTY: No, you two boys can't come in.

You have that frog.

And we don't want any frogs in here.

STEVE: What frog?

You don't see any frogs, do you?

SUE: No, we don't see any frogs.

But we just don't want you to come in.

13

STEVE: I know what we can do.

Sh! Don't make any noise.

We can't go in there.

But the frog can.

JOE: I thought of doing that.

The girls will really be scared.

They don't like frogs.

14

BETTY: Help! Help!

It's that frog, Sue.

Get it away from here.

SUE: Wait, Betty. Don't be scared.

This is just a toy frog.

And don't be scared of real frogs.

All they can do is jump and croak.

BETTY: Steve and Joe scared me.

That wasn't a nice thing to do.

SUE: I know what we can do, Betty.

The boys will want this frog back.

Then they will get a surprise.

Come with me!

We'll get something from my house.

Two Frogs?

BETTY: This is going to be fun.

Now we can scare Joe and Steve!

Wait and see how they run!

SUE: Hi, Joe. Hi, Steve.

Are you looking for something?

STEVE: Yes, we're looking for Joe's frog.

Is it in that box?

17

JOE: My toy frog scared you, didn't it?

You thought it was a real one.

BETTY: It really did surprise me.

SUE: Here's the box.

STEVE: Look in the box, Joe.

Did the girls put the frog back?

BETTY: You'll find a frog in there.

We don't want your frog.

BETTY: Come back! Come back!

Don't you want your toy frog?

SUE: How do you like being scared?

JOE: I wasn't really scared.

Just a little surprised.

Boys aren't scared of frogs.

BETTY: Not much!

21

Lucy Didn't Listen

Lucy was a busy worker.

She painted a lot of nice pictures.

She was a good reader.

And she liked to put things away.

But Lucy had one problem.

She did not listen.

One day Lucy was busy painting.

Mrs. Day said, "Put your work away.
We have to go to the library now."

But Lucy didn't listen.
She was too busy painting.

Lucy looked up from the painting.

She saw the boys and girls going out.

"I'll have to stop painting," she thought.

"We are going to lunch now.

I'll get my lunch."

Mary saw Lucy with her lunch bag.

"What are you doing with that?" she said.

"Are your library books in there?"

"No," said Lucy.

"I thought we were going to lunch."

Mrs. Day looked at Lucy and said,
"Oh, Lucy! You didn't listen.
I said that we were going to the library."

Lucy said, "I do listen, Mrs. Day.
Today I was too busy painting.
I didn't hear you."

"You'll have to go back to the room,"
said Mrs. Day.
"Get your library book.
Then come to the library."

Lucy's Too Busy

Mary saw Lucy come into the library.

Lucy had her book and her lunch bag.

"You didn't put your lunch bag away," said Mary.

"I was much too busy getting my book," said Lucy.

Lucy looked for a good book to read.
She wanted a book about animals.

"Do you all have your books now?"
said Mrs. Day.

"Yes, Mrs. Day," said all the children
but Lucy.
Lucy didn't hear Mrs. Day.
She was too busy reading her book.

"After we get back to the room,
we'll go out to play," said Mrs. Day.

Jim said, "Lucy's back in the library.
She was reading when I saw her.
Do you want me to get her?"

"Yes, please. Tell her to come with us,"
said Mrs. Day.

Jim went to get Lucy.

When she and Jim got back to the room,
the children were going out.

Lucy and Jim went out, too.

Lucy had her lunch bag and her book.

"Did you forget to put
your things away?" said Charlie.

But Lucy didn't hear him.
She was too busy reading a story.

Lucy was busy reading when Mary said,

"Let's play SQUIRREL IN THE TREE."

Jim went over to Lucy and said,

"Come on, Lucy.

Please be a squirrel in this tree."

He put Lucy with two children.

Then Mrs. Day said,

"Run, squirrels, run!"

But Lucy didn't run.

Charlie said, "Run, Lucy, run!

Please listen, will you?

Run to that tree over there!"

"I'm listening," said Lucy.

"I can run over to that tree."

And she did!

Mary looked over at Lucy.

"Oh, Lucy!" she said.

"You didn't listen at all.

We didn't want you to run

to the real tree!"

Where's Lucy?

The children had fun playing.

When the time for play was over,

they went back to the room to work.

Then Mrs. Day said,

"We're going to Room 2.

We will see a puppet play there.

Please put your work away now."

But where was Lucy?

In the workroom!

She was putting her things away.

She didn't hear what Mrs. Day said.

After Lucy had put the things away,
she went back into the big room.

"No one is here," she thought.
"Where did the others go?
They didn't go out to play.
And they didn't go to the library.
I know! They went to eat lunch!
I'll get my lunch bag!"

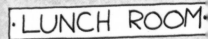

Lucy went to the lunchroom.

But the others were not there.

"Where could they all be?"
thought Lucy.

"It can't be time to eat now.

I'll have to go back to the room.

They all went somewhere without me."

Lucy went back to her room.

"I don't know what to do now,"
thought Lucy.

"I'm scared in this big room."

Just then Mrs. Day walked in.

"Here you are, Lucy!" she said.

"I have looked and looked for you.

I couldn't find you."

"I thought you were eating.
Where were you?" said Lucy.

"I said that we were going
to a puppet play," said Mrs. Day.

"Oh, good!" said Lucy.
"I like plays!"

"You may not get to see the play, Lucy.
It may be all over," said Mrs. Day.

Lucy and Mrs. Day went to Room 2.

"Oh, my!" said Lucy.

"Is this the end?"

"You weren't listening, Lucy,"
said Mrs. Day.

"And you didn't get to see the play.

It was a play about goats."

"I couldn't hear you.

I was busy in the workroom," said Lucy.

"I had to put my things away."

"You are much too busy to listen,"
said Mrs. Day.

"That is your problem, Lucy."

"This wasn't a good day for me
at all," said Lucy.

"I'm not going to be too busy
to listen any more!"

Pictures and Print

A picture may help you to read
a sentence the way someone said it.

In the picture John likes the color
he just painted the doghouse.
Read what John said:

What a color for a doghouse!

In the same picture Billy is not
pleased with the color John painted it.
Read what Billy said:

What a color for a doghouse!

The words in the sentences are alike.

Did the sentences sound alike
when you read them?

Sometimes the print will help you
to read a sentence the way it was said.

I'm

Come and HELP me!

You're going.

Sometimes there are no pictures.

Sometimes the way it is printed
will not help you.

See if you know how to read this:

My big golden cat plays that he's
a tiger.

The house is a jungle to him.

Mother tells him, "Get out of there!"

But the golden tiger hunts
where he likes.

The Three Billy Goats

Puppets for the Play

You are going to read a play

about three billy goats.

You can make puppets for this play.

Make a big, big puppet to be

Big, Big Billy Goat.

Make a big puppet to be
Big Billy Goat.

Make a little puppet to be
Little Billy Goat.

Make a scary-looking puppet to be
the troll.

The mean troll may have big teeth
for eating billy goats!

You can make a bridge.

Put a sign on the end of it.

On the sign put TROLL'S BRIDGE.

The bridge will hide the troll.

The goats will go over the bridge.

Have someone be the noisemaker.

He will make the foot noises

for the billy goats.

THE PLAY

TROLL: I am a mean troll.

And this is my bridge.

I'm happy to have you here.

You can come onto my bridge

any time you want.

But when you do, I'll eat you up!

Ha, ha, ha!

LITTLE BILLY GOAT: Oh, I see

some nice green grass over there.

I'll just go over that bridge

and get some.

NOISEMAKER: (MAKE LITTLE FOOT NOISES.)

 TROLL: What's all that noise on my bridge?

 LITTLE BILLY GOAT: It's Little Billy Goat.

I'm going to get some nice green grass.

It's on that hillside over there.

 TROLL: When you go over my bridge,

I'll eat you up!

I'm a mean troll! Ha, ha, ha!

LITTLE BILLY GOAT: Oh, no! I'm too little to eat.

Wait for Big Billy Goat.

He will want some of that grass.

He'll be coming over your bridge.

TROLL: Get out of here, then,

before I eat the two of you.

NOISEMAKER: (MAKE LITTLE FOOT NOISES.)

BIG BILLY GOAT: Oh, Little Billy Goat is eating on that hillside.

The grass looks better over there.

I want some before he eats it all.

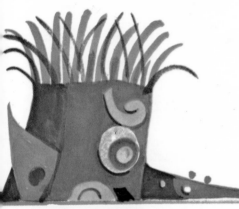

TROLL: What's making that noise
on my bridge?

BIG BILLY GOAT: I am Big Billy Goat.
I'm going to the hillside.

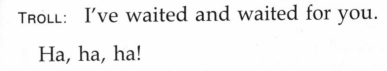

TROLL: I've waited and waited for you.
Ha, ha, ha!
You'll make a nice big lunch for me.

BIG BILLY GOAT: Oh, no!

Don't eat me up.

I'm not very big.

But Big, Big Billy Goat is on his way.

And I can hear him coming.

TROLL: Then get away from here

before I put an end to you.

NOISEMAKER: (MAKE BIG FOOT NOISES.)

BIG, BIG BILLY GOAT: Oh, my!

Little Billy Goat and Big Billy Goat

are eating that nice green grass.

I want some, too.

TROLL: What's all that noise up there?

BIG, BIG BILLY GOAT: I'm

Big, Big Billy Goat.

I'm going to that hillside

to get some nice green grass.

TROLL: Oh, no, you're not.

I've waited and waited for you.

I'm going to eat you up!

53

BIG, BIG BILLY GOAT: Get out
of my way, you old troll!
You didn't eat Little Billy Goat.
You didn't eat Big Billy Goat.
And you're not going to eat me!

TROLL: I let the two of them go.
I was waiting for a big lunch!
And you're it!

BIG, BIG BILLY GOAT: Take that!

TROLL: Let me go. I won't eat you.
I won't! Please, let me go.

BIG, BIG BILLY GOAT: That's more like it.
You get away from here now.

TROLL: But I can't go away.
This bridge is my home.

BIG, BIG BILLY GOAT: It's my bridge now.
You go find another bridge.
And don't come back here.
Take your sign and go!

BIG, BIG BILLY GOAT: I'm a big, big old
billy goat.
You can come onto my bridge
any time you want.
And—
I won't eat you up!

TOO MANY
BOZOS

by Lilian Moore

"Mother," said Danny.

"May I have a dog?"

Danny's mother looked at him.

"Danny," she said.

"You asked me that two days ago.

And what did I say?"

"No," said Danny.

"You asked me the day before that, too," said Danny's mother.

"And what did I say to you?"

"No," said Danny.

Danny's mother said, "No, Danny! This house is too little for a dog."

"But I have a good name for a dog," said Danny.

"I want to name him Bozo."

"NO, Danny!" said Danny's mother.

And Danny knew it was time to stop.

Danny ran out to the park to play.

He played in the park with Pete.

Then Danny saw the little frog.

Danny wanted that frog for a pet.

Pete helped him get it.

They got a box and put the frog
into it.

Then Danny took the frog home.

"Oh, boy!" Danny said to the frog.

"Am I happy to have you.

Won't Mom be surprised!"

Mom was surprised.

"Now I have a pet,"
Danny said to his mother.

"Do you want to take him?"

"No, thanks," said Danny's mother.

Bozo the Frog

"I'm going to name my pet Bozo,"
Danny said.

"Bozo the Frog."

"Please tell Bozo the Frog
not to come out of your room,"
said Danny's mother.

Danny took Bozo the Frog to his room.
He took good care of him.
He made a nice home for him
and got him some good things to eat.

What fun the frog was!

And what a good jumper!

Danny put down one book.

Bozo jumped right over it.

Danny put down two books, then three.

And Bozo jumped over them all!

One day Bozo made one jump too many.

Jump! Bozo was out of his house.

Jump! Jump!

He was out of Danny's room.

Jump! Jump! Jump!

He was here and there,
all over the house.

Then Bozo saw something he liked.

He jumped right into it!

Danny's mother had just come in
to do her work.

"Oh, no!" she cried when she saw Bozo.

Bozo was scared!

He jumped right at Danny's mother.

"A frog!" cried Danny's mother.

"Danny, take that frog
out of this house right now!"

Danny put Bozo into the box
and walked back to the park.

On the way to the park,

Danny saw Billy.

"Look what I have!" said Billy.

"Look what I have!" said Danny.

Right then and there, they traded.

Danny ran all the way home.

"Oh, boy!" he thought.

"Am I happy I saw Billy.

Won't Mom be surprised!"

Bozo the Mouse

Mom was surprised.

Danny let her see

what was in the box.

There was a little mouse in it.

"This is my new pet," Danny said.

"I'm going to name him Bozo.

Bozo the Mouse."

Danny took the mouse out
and let it walk on his arm.

"Look, Mom!" he cried.

"See what Bozo can do!

Do you want him to walk

on your arm?"

"No, thanks!" said Danny's mother.

"And Danny, don't let that mouse

out of your room!"

"It's all right, Mom," said Danny.

"Bozo the Mouse won't get out."

Danny took good care of Bozo the Mouse.

He played with him a lot.

But one day Bozo got out.

He got out of Danny's room!

"Sniff, sniff!" went Bozo the Mouse.

Danny's mother had just made a cake.

Bozo the Mouse saw the cake.

And he liked it very much.

When Danny's mother took a good look
at her cake, she cried, "My cake!
Oh, my nice cake!
Danny, take that cake-eating mouse
out of this house right now."

Danny was not happy.
He put Bozo the Mouse into his box.

"I'll have to take Bozo the Mouse
back to the pet store," he thought.
"That's where Billy got him."

Danny took Bozo to the pet store.

The pet store man was happy to get
the mouse back.

Danny and the pet store man
made a trade.

Danny ran all the way home.

"Oh, boy!" he thought.

"Am I happy I went to the pet store!

What will Mom say when she sees
what I have now?"

Danny's mother did not say anything —
not right away.

She just looked at the box.

Then she asked, "WHAT IS THAT?"

"This is an ant farm," Danny said.

"See all the ants?"

"Ants!" cried Danny's mother.

"I can just see ants
all over the house.

No ants, Danny! Do you hear me?"

"Mother," said Danny.

"I just have to have a pet."

"Yes," said Danny's mother.

"I can see that you do!

I know just the pet for you."

73

"Is it better than a frog?"
asked Danny.

"Much better," said his mother.

"Is it better than a mouse?"
asked Danny.

"Much, much better," said his mother.

"Is it better than an ant farm?"
asked Danny.

"Oh, yes!" said his mother.
"Much, much, much better!"

"Danny," she said.

"How would you like a dog?"

"A DOG!" cried Danny. "A DOG!"

"A little dog," said Danny's mother.

"Oh, boy!" said Danny.
"Do you know what I'm going
to name him?"

"Bozo," said Danny. "Bozo the Dog."

"Bozo!" said Danny's mother.
"What a surprise!"

I WOULDN'T

by John Ciardi

There's a mouse house

In the hall wall

With a small door

By the hall floor

Where the fat cat

Sits all day,

Sits that way

All day

Every day

Just to say,

"Come out and play"

To the nice mice

In the hall wall

With the small door

By the hall floor.

And do they

Come out and play

When the fat cat

Asks them to?

Well, would you?

More Than One Way

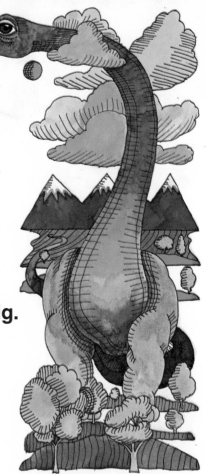

You can say many things in more than just one way.

Sometimes one word may be better than another.

Read the words that tell about the picture of the dinosaur.

You know other words that mean **big.**

Giant is a word that tells how very big the dinosaur is.

What other words could tell better about the pictures you see here?

the **big** dinosaur

the **mean** dog

the **little** mouse

the **noisy** frog

RED GOLD

RED GOLD

BUZZY BEAR
and the
RAINBOW

BY

DOROTHY MARINO

One day Buzzy Bear ran out to play.

It had just stopped raining.

Buzzy stopped by a tree.

"Oh, look!" he cried to a bird

in a tree.

"There's a rainbow."

"Yes, I know," said the bird.

"They say there's gold at the end
of the rainbow.

But you have to get there
before it goes away."

Buzzy didn't wait to hear more.

He ran home.

Mother and Father Bear were looking
at the rainbow, too.

CORN   BEANS   PEAS   MARSH-MALLOWS   BUBBLE GUM

Buzzy ran into the house
to get a big pot.

When he had come back out, he said,
"I'm going to get the gold."
Then he ran on.

"That's just a story,"
called Mother Bear.

"Gold would not do us any good,"
called Father Bear.

Buzzy just ran on.

He could see the end of the rainbow
by a big rock.

When Buzzy got to the big rock,
he couldn't see the rainbow.

A squirrel was there.

"I'm looking for the end
of the rainbow," said Buzzy
to the squirrel.

"Look at the bushes over there,"
said the squirrel.

"There's the end of the rainbow."

Buzzy ran to find it.

The squirrel called after him,
"If you're looking for the gold,
that's just a story."

Buzzy just ran on.

When he got to the bushes,
he couldn't see the rainbow.

A rabbit was there.

"I'm looking for the end
of the rainbow," said Buzzy
to the rabbit.

86

"See that grass over there?"
the rabbit said.
"There's the end of the rainbow."

Buzzy ran to find it.

The rabbit called after him,
"If you're looking for the gold,
that's just a story."

Buzzy just ran on.
When he got to the grass,
he couldn't see the rainbow.
A chipmunk was there.

"I'm looking for the end
of the rainbow," said Buzzy
to the chipmunk.

"Look at that big tree over there,"
said the chipmunk.
"There's the end of the rainbow."

Buzzy ran to find it.
The chipmunk called after him,
"If you're looking for the gold,
that's just a story."
Buzzy just ran on.

When he got to the tree,

Buzzy looked all over.

There was no rainbow anywhere.

"This really must be the end

of the rainbow!" said Buzzy.

"I wonder if I got here in time."

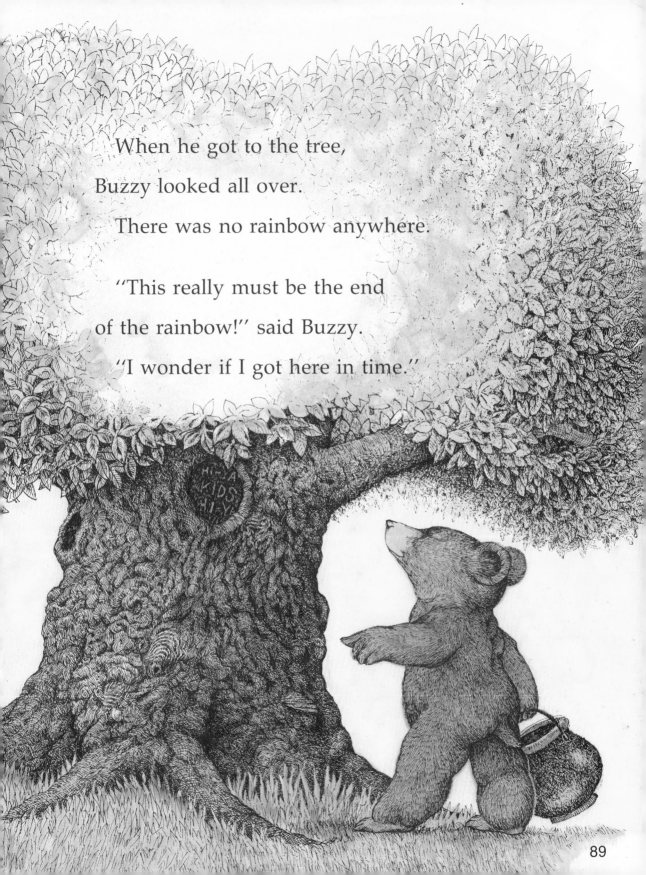

The Pot of Gold

Buzzy went up the tree.

Then he stopped.

There was a big hole in the tree.

Buzzy looked in.

"I've found it," he cried.

"I found the gold . . . and I like it."

Buzzy put the gold into the big pot.

Then he went down the tree.

"I'll run home now," thought Buzzy.

"I found the gold," Buzzy called
to the chipmunk as he ran by the grass.

"Wait, let me see," cried the chipmunk.

Buzzy just ran on.

The chipmunk ran after Buzzy.

"I found the gold," Buzzy called
to the rabbit as he ran by the bushes.

"Wait, let me see," cried the rabbit.

Buzzy just ran on ahead.

The rabbit ran after Buzzy

and the chipmunk.

"I found the gold," Buzzy called
to the squirrel as he ran
by the big rock.

"Wait, let me see," cried the squirrel.

Buzzy just ran on ahead.

The squirrel ran after Buzzy
and the chipmunk and the rabbit.

They all ran to Buzzy's house.

Buzzy Bear put the big pot down.

"Look, Mother," he cried.

"There really was gold at the end

of the rainbow."

They all looked into the pot.

"It's honey!" cried Father Bear.

"Buzzy found honey at the end
of the rainbow!"

Buzzy Bear called the little bird
from the tree.

Then Mother Bear asked all the animals
to eat supper with them.

Mother Bear made pancakes.

They put the golden honey on them.

"I'm happy Buzzy looked for the gold,"
said Mother Bear.

And Father Bear said,
"The gold that Buzzy found
is better than real gold!"

COOKING

This will be a chocolate cake,

This is a cherry pie,

This will be a doughnut

When the mud is dry.

—Myra Livingston

PEDRO'S BIKE
by Mary Lou Alsin

"Mama, Mama, can't I have a bike?" asked Pedro.

"All the boys have bikes to ride."

"How many times do I have to tell you, Pedro?

We don't have money for a bike," said Mama.

"I'll ask Manuel to wish for a bike
for me," thought Pedro.

"He's very good at wishing."

Pedro found Manuel and said,
"Manuel, I want something very much.
If you wish for it, will I get it?"

"I don't know," said Manuel.
"Sometimes the wishing I do works,
but not always."

"I could wish for something for you.

Then we could just wait and see

if the wish works," said Manuel.

"What did you want me to wish for?"

"A bike," said Pedro.

"I want a bike."

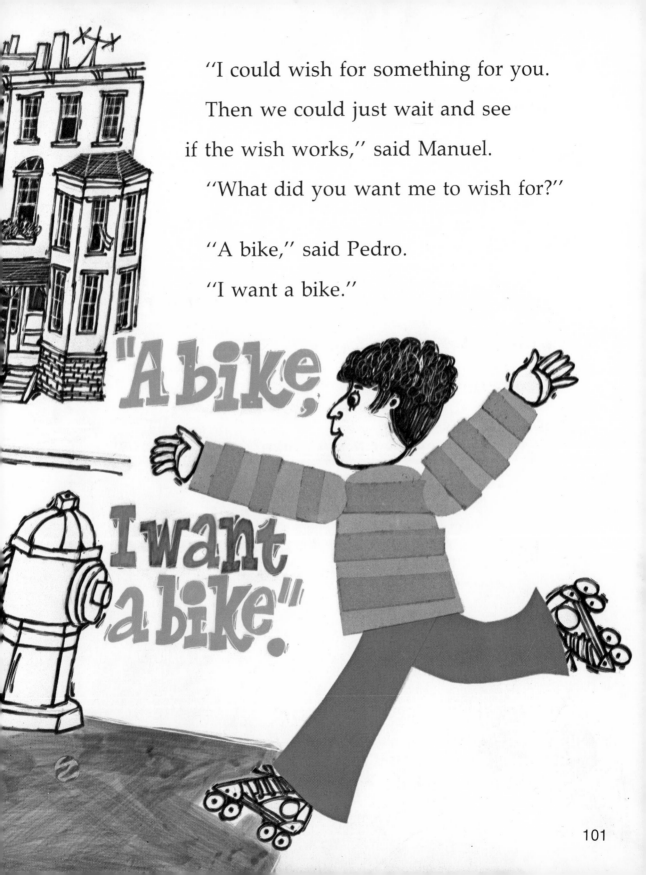

"A bike, I want a bike."

"All right," said Manuel.

"I'll wish for a bike for you.

"First I take this lucky money.

Then I put it down on a white rock

and make a wish.

"Lucky money on lucky rock,

please let Pedro have a bike."

"But I want a new bike," said Pedro.

"Could you ask for a new bike?"

"Yes," said Manuel.

"Lucky money on lucky rock,
please get Pedro a bike that's new."

"And I want the bike to be green,"
said Pedro.

"I wish you'd said that before,"
said Manuel.

And he made the wish another time.

Then Pedro said, "I want a bell on it.
And I'd like a basket for it, too."

103

Pedro Waits

"You can't wish for everything
all at one time!" cried Manuel.

"As soon as the bike comes,
I'll wish for the bell and basket."

Pedro waited all that day
for the bike, but it didn't come.

He waited day after day.
Manuel's wish wasn't working.

"My bike didn't come, Manuel,"
said Pedro.

"Would you make that wish for me
just one more time?" he asked.

"That wouldn't help any," said Manuel.
"Sometimes it takes many days
for a wish to work."

"Wait, wait, wait!" said Pedro.
"I'm sick of waiting."

Just then he looked over
at a truck that was parked
in the street.

"Look, Manuel!" cried Pedro.
"There's a wheel on that truck.
I'll make a bike."

There was a man in the truck.

Pedro ran over and asked him,
"May I have the bike wheel
that's on your truck?"

"That isn't just a bike wheel,"
said the man.

"It's an old, old bike
that someone didn't want any more."

"Didn't want?" cried Pedro.
"Wow! I want it.
Can I have it, please?"

The man got the bike down for Pedro.

"Look, Manuel!" cried Pedro.
"The bike you wished for did come."

"You wanted a new bike," said Manuel.
"How can you ever ride that?
Someone will have to fix it
before you can ride it.
I may be good at wishing.
But I'm no good at fixing things.
Maybe Mr. Lee could help you fix it."

A New Green Bike

Pedro took the bike to Mr. Lee's house.

"See my new bike," said Pedro.

"I wonder if it can be fixed.

Will you please help me?"

"I think we can fix that bike,"
said Mr. Lee.

"Let's take it down to my workroom."

"This is my lucky day," said Pedro.

When Pedro got home, he said,
"Mama! Mama! I have to tell you
about my wonderful bike!

Mr. Lee is going to help me fix it up
like new."

The next day, as soon as school was out,
Pedro ran right home.

"Mama, I want to help Mr. Lee fix
my bike.

Can I go over to his house?"

"Yes," said Mama.

Pedro found Mr. Lee taking some things
out of his truck.

"Is my bike all fixed?" asked Pedro.

"I fixed the wheels," said Mr. Lee.
"But we have a lot more to do.
As soon as I get the things out
of the truck, we'll work on the bike."

"Let me help you so that we can get to work on my bike sooner," said Pedro.

Pedro helped Mr. Lee take the things down to the workroom.

"You're a big help," said Mr. Lee. "Now we should have your bike fixed sooner than I thought we would."

Pedro and Mr. Lee didn't have much time
left to work on the bike.

Soon Pedro had to go home for supper.

The next day when Pedro came back,
Mr. Lee was doing some painting.

"Can I ride the bike now?" asked Pedro.

"No," said Mr. Lee.
"We have a little more work
to do on it."

113

"Can I help you paint?" asked Pedro.

"Yes, you can help me,"
said Mr. Lee.

As they were painting, Mr. Lee said,
"How would you like a blue bike?"

"I did want a green bike," said Pedro.

"That's no problem," said Mr. Lee.
And he put some yellow paint
and some blue paint into another can.

"Wow! Just the color I wanted!"
said Pedro.

The next day Pedro went for a ride
on his bike.

When he saw Manuel, Pedro said,
"See my wonderful new green bike."

"My wish did work after all,
didn't it?" said Manuel.

"Now can you wish
for that bell and basket?" Pedro asked.

Manuel said, "I'll wish
for your bell and basket.
But first I'm going to wish
for a bike for myself."

Saturday Night

I gave my dog a bath one day.

It was a sight to see!

I got so wet myself, I'd say

He gave the bath to me!
— Lois F. Pasley

Making One Word out of Two Words

Sometimes a new word is one
that is made of two words you know.

You know the word <u>bird</u> and you know
the word <u>house</u>.

Now you can read the word <u>birdhouse</u>.

A birdhouse is a house for birds.

The new words in the next sentences
are ones that are made of two words
you know.

Next to our schoolroom is a workroom.

At playtime it can be anywhere
we want it to be.

We can play that it is a jungle
where there are lions and tigers.

Sometimes it is scary and fun.

But when playtime is over, we put
our playthings away.

And the jungle is a workroom again.

Not a Thing to Be Scared Of

Fred and Toby liked to go fishing
with Dad.

This time they would be
out in the woods for three days.

They would stay in a little house
in the woods.

It was time for supper when they got
to the little house in the woods.

After they ate supper, Dad said,
"We'll want to get up in time
to get lots of fish.

So we must go to sleep soon."

Fred was just going to sleep
when Toby called, "Fred, I hear
water running.

There must be someone in there.
And I'm scared!"

"That's just Dad, Toby," said Fred.

"It can't be!" cried Toby.
"Dad's still right here with us."

"Get up, Dad! Get up!" called Fred.

"There's someone in there.

Someone turned on the water."

"I hear it," said Dad.

Dad got up and went to look.

"There's no one in here," he called.

"One of us must have left

the water running."

Something Outside

Soon Dad and Fred were asleep.

But not Toby!

He could hear a noise by the window.

He thought he saw two big eyes.

Now Toby was really scared!

But the next time he looked,

the eyes weren't there.

"I must be seeing things!"

thought Toby.

He waited, but no eyes came back.

Soon Toby was sleeping, too.

The next day Dad said,

"We can fix a lunch to take with us."

"I'll get the apples we left outside,"
said Fred.

When he came back in,
he looked at Toby and asked,
"Did you eat any apples last night?"

"No," said Toby.

Then Fred looked at Dad and asked,
"Did you eat any apples last night?"

Dad said, "No."

"Then who did eat them?" asked Fred.
"We had many more apples than this."

"We'd better put the apples in the house
from now on," said Dad.

Toby thought, "What next?"

"Time to go fishing!" said Dad.

"Let's be on our way, boys."

They walked to the pond.

They had two big fish by lunchtime.

"Where's our lunch?" asked Fred.

"Oh, I forgot it!" said Toby.

"I'll run back and get it."

Toby ran back to the house
and got the lunch basket.

On the way back to the pond,
he could hear a noise up in a tree.
He looked up and saw
a big bushy tail.
"My, that's a funny-looking tail
for a squirrel!" thought Toby
as he ran back to Dad and Fred.

Something Inside

When they got back to the house

that night, Fred and Toby went inside.

"Dad! Come here!" called Fred.

Dad went in and looked around.

There were cans all over the room.

The cake pan was turned over.

And right beside it was

what was left of an apple.

"Toby, did you do this
when you came back
for the lunch basket?" cried Fred.

"I didn't do this," said Toby.
"Someone must have come in
when we were out."

"I don't think anyone came in, Toby,"
said Dad.
"We're way out in the woods.
No one is anywhere around here."

"But someone must have come in.
Toby says he didn't do this.
And I know I didn't," said Fred.

"Then who did?" asked Toby.

"I really don't know," said Dad.
"From now on, I'll fix the door
so that no one can get in here."

After supper, Dad said,
"You boys turn out the light
and go right to sleep."

More Noises

Fred and Toby listened
to the night sounds.

Somewhere in the woods
there was a "Whoo! Whoo!"

"What's that?" asked Toby.

"It's just a night bird," said Fred.

Toby didn't want to tell anyone,

but he was still a little scared.

Soon Fred and Dad were asleep.

Toby could hear something.

He looked around.

There was no one at the window.

He listened carefully.

"Oh, no! Not again!" thought Toby.

He could hear water running.

He shook Dad's arm.

"What do you want?" asked Dad.

"Someone's out there!" said Toby.
"The water's running again!"

"I'll get him this time!" said Dad.
"Stay here and be still."

Dad got up without making any noise.

He got his flashlight.

When he got to the doorway,
he turned on the flashlight.

Dad laughed and said,
"Come here, boys!

I want you to see what I see!

Someone's having a good time
with our leftover fish!"

In the bright light of the flashlight
they could see an animal.

"A raccoon!" cried Fred.

"I think that's the funny-looking
squirrel I saw up in a tree," said Toby.

"That must be who ate our apples!"
Fred said.
"But he couldn't turn
the water on by himself, could he, Dad?"

"Yes, he could," said Dad.

"Raccoons are bright animals,
and they like to put things
in the water before eating them."

"How did he get into the house?"
asked Toby.

"Just the way he's getting out,"
said Dad.

"Now let's all get some sleep.
There's not a thing to be scared of."

The City

Come to the city.

Everywhere you look you see

big buildings and lots of people.

Where are all the people going?

What sounds do you hear in the city?

Have you seen a big city?

Tell what you saw and what you did

in the big city.

More Than One Meaning

You know that a word can have more than one meaning.

You have to think of the meaning that goes with the other words in the sentence.

Look at the picture.

Here are two sentences.

1. There isn't **room** for another pet in this house.

2. I do not have a pet in my **room.**

One of them goes with the picture.
Can you find the right sentence?

140

Can you find the right sentences
for the pictures here?

1. The ants are more than a **foot** away.

2. The ants are walking over my **foot.**

1. You will have to **sign** this card
   before you take out an animal book.

2. The **sign** says that I can find
   an animal book here.

Ants live here
by the curb stone,
see?
They worry a lot
about giants like
me.

— *Lilian Moore*

142

BLUE GRASS

BLUE GRASS

WAIT FOR A WINDY DAY

by LILIAN MOORE

There was something

that Red Fox wanted.

It was something he wanted very much.

Every day he ran out of the woods

to look at Farmer Dilly's chicken house.

Every day he thought,

"How I would like a nice chicken to eat!"

Red Fox could see

the nice fat chickens.

He could smell the nice fat chickens.

But he could not get

into the chicken house to take one.

Not with Old Trooper around.

Trooper was Farmer Dilly's

big old dog.

Every time Red Fox headed
for the chicken house, Trooper ran
after him.

Every time Trooper ran after him,
Red Fox went back to the woods.

Sometimes Farmer Dilly came out
of the house after Red Fox.

Red Fox always ran away
as fast as he could.

But the next day, back he would come.
And Old Trooper would still be there
waiting.

"That old dog knows.

He always knows,"

thought Red Fox one day.

"It must be that he smells me.

That's it!

He smells my fox smell when I come out

of the woods."

Red Fox thought and thought.

Then he laughed.

"I know what I can do," he thought.

"I can take care of that old dog!"

Red Fox looked around
for some big bones.

He looked for good big bones
that a big old dog would like.

"I'll wait for a windy day,"
said Red Fox.

"Then I will let that dog have
something to smell that is not a fox."

He laughed and thought
of the nice fat chicken
that he would get.

At last a day came that was just right.

The wind made wooshing noises
in the trees.

It made wooshing noises in the bushes.

Mrs. Dilly said, "This is
a nice windy day.
This is a good day
to put my wash out."

She put out Farmer Dilly's
brown overalls and his blue overalls.
Then she put out his old brown shirt
and his good white one.

"There!" said Mrs. Dilly.
"Now all my wash is out."
She was pleased.

Red Fox was pleased, too.

He sniffed the wind.

"Just the right day," he thought.

He took the big bones
and put them in the woods.

"That dog will have a good time
in the woods today!" laughed Red Fox.

"And I will have a good time
in the chicken house!"

This time Red Fox did not come
out of the woods.

This time he just waited.

The wind blew the trees.

Soon it blew the good smell of bones
right to Old Trooper's nose.

Sniff, sniff! Trooper came running.

His nose was down. Sniff, sniff, sniff.

The wind was full of the smell

of good big bones.

Sniff! Trooper ran into the woods.

"Now!" thought Red Fox.

"Now for the chicken house!"

Red Fox ran out of the woods.

All he had to do now was run

to the chicken house.

Red Fox ran to where

Mrs. Dilly had put out her wash.

Red Fox Gets Away

Red Fox stopped.

What was that?

Arms and legs were all around him.

Here and there and everywhere

arms and legs were going up and down.

"Oh, my!" thought Red Fox.

"Farmer Dilly went to get help.

Now all of the farmers are after me!

I've got to get out of here!"

Red Fox ran and ran.

"All of the farmers were after me,"

thought Red Fox.

"But I got away!

I got away from them all."

Red Fox never did go back
to Farmer Dilly's chicken house.

Old Trooper still looked for the fox
every day.

"I know he will not come back,"
thought Old Trooper.

"He's afraid of me."

Farmer Dilly still looked
for the fox, too.

"I know he won't come back,"
thought Farmer Dilly.

"He's afraid of me."

How surprised they would be
if they knew what really scared
Red Fox away!

The *ed* Ending

Think of what you know

about the sounds for **ed** endings

as you read this story.

I make three sounds.

Never Go Fishing with a Porcupine

Raccoon liked fish better
than anything.

"But fishing for supper takes
too much time," he thought.

Just then, Porcupine walked by.

Raccoon had a very good idea.

"Porcupine, you can help me get
a good fish supper for us tonight,"
he called.

Porcupine looked surprised,
but he was pleased.

He didn't know how he could help,
but he did want some fish.

So the two of them went to the pond.

Raccoon waited, and when Porcupine
was right beside the water,
PUSH went Raccoon!

And SPLASH went Porcupine
into the water!

Porcupine was surprised and then
he was scared!

"Oh, help!" he cried.

Raccoon got a stick.

"Take this, Porcupine!" he cried.

And he helped Porcupine out
of the water.

Sticking to Porcupine's back were
three big fish!

"It worked! My idea worked!"
said Raccoon, as he laughed.

"You had the good idea,
but I have the fish," said Porcupine.

"If you're having any supper tonight,
you'd better get busy."

Porcupine smiled and walked away.

"You scared all the fish!"
Raccoon called after him.

But Porcupine just turned and said,
"Who scared the fish away?"

Little Raccoon
and the
Thing in the Pool

by

Lilian Moore

Little Raccoon was little
but he was brave.

One day Mother Raccoon said,
"Tonight the moon will be out.
It will be bright and full.
Can you go to the pool
all by yourself, Little Raccoon?
Can you get some fish for supper?"

"Oh, yes, yes!" said Little Raccoon.
"I'll get the best fish
you ever ate."

Little Raccoon was little
but he was brave.

That night the moon came up
big and full and very bright.

"Go now, Little Raccoon,"
said his mother.
"Walk to the pool.
You will see a big tree
that makes a bridge over the pool.
Walk over the pool on the tree.
The best place to get fish
is on the other side."

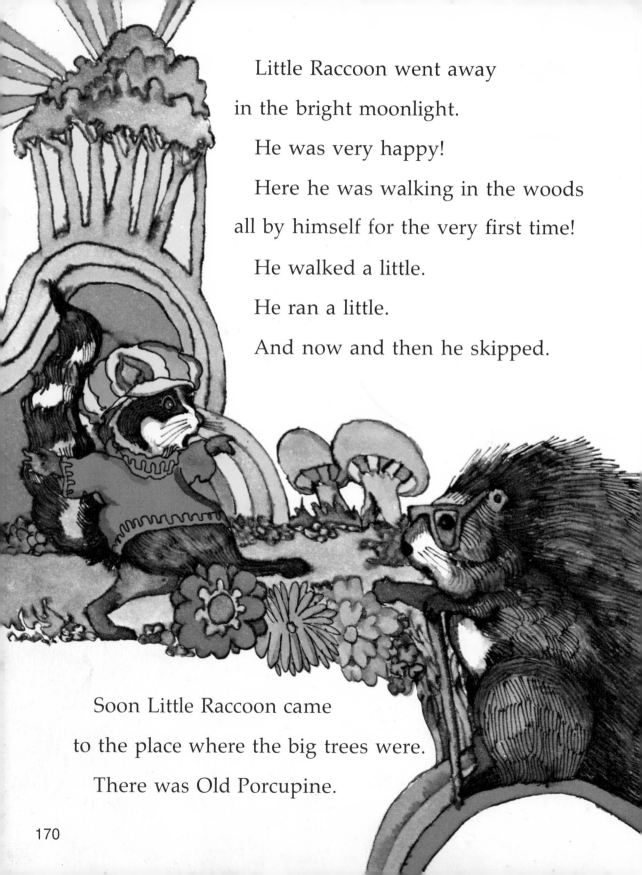

Little Raccoon went away
in the bright moonlight.

He was very happy!

Here he was walking in the woods
all by himself for the very first time!

He walked a little.

He ran a little.

And now and then he skipped.

Soon Little Raccoon came
to the place where the big trees were.

There was Old Porcupine.

Old Porcupine was surprised
to see Little Raccoon walking
in the woods without his mother.
   "Where are you going,
all by yourself?" asked Old Porcupine.

   "To the pool," said Little Raccoon.
   "I'm going to get some fish
for supper."

   "Be careful, Little Raccoon,"
said Old Porcupine.
   "You don't have what I have,
you know!"

"I'm not afraid,"
said Little Raccoon.

He was little but he was brave.

Little Raccoon went on
in the bright moonlight.
He walked a little.
He ran a little.
And now and then he skipped.

Soon he came to the place
where the green grass was.
There was Big Skunk.

172

Big Skunk was surprised, too,
to see Little Raccoon walking
in the woods without his mother.

"Where are you going,
all by yourself?" asked Big Skunk.

"To the pool," said Little Raccoon.
"I'm going to get some fish
for supper."

"Be careful, Little Raccoon,"
said Big Skunk.
"You don't have what I have,
you know!"

173

"I'm not afraid,"
said Little Raccoon, and he went on.

Soon he saw Fat Rabbit.
Fat Rabbit was sleeping,
but he opened one eye.
Then he jumped up.
"My, you scared me!" he said.
"Where are you going,
all by yourself, Little Raccoon?"

"I'm going to the pool,"
said Little Raccoon.

"Way over there on the other side
of the pool."

"OOOOOH!" said Fat Rabbit.
"Aren't you afraid of IT?"

"Afraid of what?"
asked Little Raccoon.

"Of the thing in the pool!"
said Fat Rabbit. "I am!"

"I'm not!" said Little Raccoon,
and he went on.

The Thing in the Pool

Soon Little Raccoon came
to the big tree
that was over the pool.

"This is where I cross,"
said Little Raccoon to himself.

"And over there on the other side
is where I get the fish."

Little Raccoon walked onto the tree
and began to cross the pool.

He was brave, but he did wish
he had not seen Fat Rabbit.

He did not want to think about IT.

He did not want to think
about the thing in the pool.

But he couldn't help it.

He just had to stop and look.

There was something in the pool!

There it was,

in the bright moonlight,

looking up at him!

Little Raccoon did not want it

to know that he was afraid.

He made a face.

The thing in the pool

made a face, too.

And what a mean face it was!

Little Raccoon was scared.

He ran away!

He ran past Fat Rabbit
and scared him.

He ran and ran and did not stop
until he saw Big Skunk.

"What is it? What is it?"
asked Big Skunk.

"There's a big thing in the pool!"
said Little Raccoon.
"I can't get past it!"

"Do you want me to go with you?"
asked Big Skunk.
"I can make it go away."

179

"Oh, no, no!" said Little Raccoon.
"You don't have to do that!"

"Then you'll have to take a rock
with you," said Big Skunk.
"Just show that thing in the pool
that you have a rock!"

Little Raccoon did want
to get some good fish.
He took a rock and walked back
to the pool.

"Maybe the thing went away,"
Little Raccoon said to himself.

But no.

When he looked down into the pool,
there it was!

Little Raccoon did not want to show
that he was afraid.

He let the thing in the pool see
that he had a rock.

But the thing in the pool
had a rock, too.

And what a big rock it was!

A Stick This Time

Little Raccoon was brave
but he was little.

He ran like anything.

He ran and ran,
and he did not stop
until he saw Old Porcupine.

"What is it? What is it?"
asked Old Porcupine.

Little Raccoon told him
about the thing in the pool.

"He had a rock, too,"
said Little Raccoon.
"A big BIG rock!"

"Then you must have a stick
this time," said Old Porcupine.

"Go back and show that thing
that you have a big stick!"

Little Raccoon did want
to get some good fish.

He took a stick and walked back
to the pool.

"Maybe this time it went away,"
Little Raccoon said to himself.

But no.

The thing in the pool was still there.

Little Raccoon did not wait.

He showed the thing in the pool his big stick.

But the thing in the pool had a stick, too.

A big BIG stick.

Little Raccoon turned and ran.

He ran and ran past Fat Rabbit —

past Big Skunk —

past Old Porcupine —

and he did not stop until he was home.

Back to the Pond

Little Raccoon told his mother
all about the thing in the pool.

"Oh, Mother," he said,
"I wanted to go for fish
all by myself.

I wanted to get good fish
for supper!"

"And you will!" said Mother Raccoon.
"Go back to the pool, Little Raccoon.
But this time do not make a face.
Do not take a rock.
Do not take a stick."

"But what can I do?"
asked Little Raccoon.

"Just smile," said Mother Raccoon.
"This time just smile at the thing
in the pool."

"Is that all?" asked Little Raccoon.
"Are you sure?"

"That is all," said his mother.
"I am sure."

Little Raccoon was brave,
and his mother was sure!

He went all the way back to the pool.

"Maybe the thing went away at last,"
he said to himself.

But no.

There it was!

Little Raccoon made himself look down
into the pool.

Then he made himself smile
at the thing in the pool.

The thing in the pool smiled back!

Little Raccoon was happy!
He began to laugh.
The thing in the pool began
to laugh, too, just like
a happy raccoon.

"Now it wants to be friends,"
said Little Raccoon to himself.
"Now I can cross!"
And he ran on the tree
to the other side of the pool.

Little Raccoon began to look

for fish in the pool.

Soon he had all the fish he wanted.

He ran back across the pool.

This time Little Raccoon waved
to the thing in the pool.
The thing in the pool waved back!

Little Raccoon went home
with the fish as fast as he could go.
It was the best fish
he and Mother Raccoon ever ate.

"I can go by myself any time,"
said Little Raccoon.

"I'm not afraid of the thing
in the pool now."

"I know," said Mother Raccoon.

"The thing in the pool isn't mean
at all!" said Little Raccoon.

"I know," said Mother Raccoon.

Little Raccoon looked at his mother.
"Tell me," he said.
"What is the thing in the pool?"

Mother Raccoon began to laugh.
Then she told him.

MY COLOR GAME

When I'm inside on a stormy day,
I have a game I like to play.
I think of colors of things I know,
Like YELLOW for the sunlight's glow.

I think of other colors, too:
PURPLE eggplant, blue-jay BLUE
Sometimes I think of things all RED,
Like fire engines or jam on bread.

Sometimes I just decide to think
Of ORANGE for the juice I drink,
But other times I think of GREEN
For stems and grass and frogs I've seen.

And so at last I have a kind
Of made-up rainbow in my mind.

Vivian Gouled